Help
Mr. Horse

by Carrie Waters
illustrated by Reggie Holladay

 HOUGHTON MIFFLIN   BOSTON

Printed in China

ISBN-13: 978-0-547-01683-2
ISBN-10: 0-547-01683-2

8 9 10 0940 16 15 14 13
4500408670

"You can all help me,"
said Mr. Horse.

Mr. Horse said,
"You can help.
You can pass out
the books."

"You can help,"
said Mr. Horse.
"You can pass out
the paper."

"And you can
pass out the pencils."

"You can
pick up the crayons,"
said Mr. Horse.

"And you can
pick up the blocks."

"I like to help,"
Little <mark>Elephant</mark> said.

"Little Elephant,"
said Mr. Horse.
"You can help, too.
You can help us have fun."

And Little Elephant
did help!

Responding

Understanding Characters Who are the characters in this story? Where are they? What are they doing?

✏ Write About It

Text to Text What other books have you read that have talking animals? Draw a picture of one of the animals. Label the animal in your picture.

WORDS TO KNOW

like

LEARN MORE WORDS

elephant | horse

✔ **TARGET SKILL** **Understanding Characters** Tell more about characters.

✔ **TARGET STRATEGY** **Infer/Predict** Use text clues to figure out more about story parts.

GENRE **Fiction** is a story that is made up.